30 Things
Twin Tells

Dr. Amber Goodman & Dr. Ashley Goodman

Copyright © 2022 Amber Goodman and Ashley Goodman

All rights reserved.

No part of this book may be reproduced, or stored in a retrieval system, or transmitted in any form or by any means, electronic, mechanical, photocopying, recording, or otherwise, without the express written permission of the publisher. For permissions and to discover more about the authors, visit www.goodmantwins.com.

The opinions expressed in this book are those of the authors and do not constitute medical advice or legal advice. Any similarities to real persons other than the authors, living or dead, are coincidental and not intended by the authors.

The authors are ordained ministers and thereby cite The Holy Bible in a sermonic and instructional capacity. All scriptures and biblical citations are intended for and reproduced for ministerial education purposes. The authors make no intellectual property claims regarding any specific translations of The Holy Bible cited herein.

ISBN-13: 979-8-218-11976-8

Printed in the United States of America

Foreword

My name is Overseer Prophet Daniel Powell, Sr. Being in ministry for over 30 years has afforded me the opportunity of encountering some extraordinary people. My spiritual daughters, Drs. Amber and Ashley Goodman, are two of those people. They are both prophetesses who are confirmed authors in their own rights. Being an established author myself, I have been afforded the opportunity to travel, preach, and teach the Gospel of Jesus Christ across nations.

I have established churches in the Philippines, Germany, and all across the United States of America. I graduated from the School of the Prophets in 2014, and I have successfully completed courses in biblical studies. I met Drs. Amber and Ashley Goodman in 2018 during a revival in Jacksonville, FL.

They began to visit Heaven to Earth Worship Center located in Tampa, FL a short while later. On one of these visits, the Lord gave me a prophetic word for the two of them, and I knew then by the word of prophecy that they were chosen by the Lord Jesus Christ as prophetesses, authors, and businesswomen.

Their assignment would be to live in God's kingdom and preach the Word of God. Because of the anointing and grace on their lives, the Lord proclaimed their powerful anointing would impact the earth through the writing of books. On that night of the revival, I saw God Himself anoint them and change the course of their lives forever! This book written by the Goodman twins was written by the power of the Holy Spirit.

As I read this spirit-filled book that talks about how to declare the kingdom of heaven on earth and how we should live a life of righteousness and holiness in God's Kingdom on earth, I was filled with a spirit of joy and purpose. As I read *30 Things: Twin Tells*, my spirit smiled, and I was so blessed. It allowed me to understand how the twins live in the Kingdom of God while walking in the power of the Holy Spirit.

I am so inspired by how they minister through their writing about salvation. I boast with confidence and assurance that Author Prophetess Dr. Amber Goodman and Author Prophetess Dr. Ashley Goodman's spirit-filled book, *30 Things: Twin Tells*, will lead readers on a mission in the word of God. Personally, it took me on a supernatural walk with the Holy Spirit into God's Kingdom with the Lord Jesus Christ through His word and by His peace.

I truly encourage everyone to buy Author Prophetess Dr. Amber Goodman's and Author Prophetess Dr. Ashley Goodman's books *A Double Portion to Know Him, Abba Father & Me: A Daily Devotional,* and *The Outcast Pharmacist*. From the time the reader begins with the first thing the twins tell and reaches the thirtieth thing that is essential to spiritual growth with their Lord God Jehovah, His Son Jesus Christ, and the Holy Spirit, there will be an increase of faith and strength that has never been imagined, witnessed, or experienced.

Overseer Prophet Daniel Powell, Sr.
With love from Prophetess Esther Powell
Faith & Works Outreach Ministries, Int. | Heaven to Earth Worship Center

Dedication

This book is dedicated to the Holy Spirit. Without Him, nothing we write would be complete. We thank You.

Introduction

This text of writing is not like a regular book. It is infused with wisdom, not in *fancy* words but power through the leading of the Holy Spirit. This writing is meant to be simple, not complex, and to be imparted into readers' lives. What we mean by this is that it will not have a layout or format of chapters. It will consist of revelations and *tells,* which means to communicate information to someone by spoken or written words. This is a form of how the Lord has called us to prophesy His word and messages.

We pray that the writing of this text will refresh your soul and ignite light into your life. It was given to us directly from heavenly wisdom and our experiences as we come to the age of 30. Thirty is usually the age when one comes into full maturity both physically and mentally to handle major and significant responsibilities. Thirty biblically represents one's dedication to a calling or task. Jesus began His ministry at the age of 30. We hope the *30 things* we will be providing and sharing information about in written form will bless you.

Contents

Foreword	3
Dedication	5
Introduction	6
Contents	7
1 | Salvation	8
2 | Care	10
3 | Gifts	12
4 | Leadership	13
5 | Love	16
6 | Words	17
7 | Wisdom	18
8 | Forgiveness	20
9 | Pure in Heart	21
10 | Stewardship	22
11 | Give Thanks, Be Thankful	23
12 | Covetousness, Envy, and Jealousy	24
13 | Our Circle	26
14 | Healing	27
15 | Tithes and Offering	29
16 | Sowing (Giving)	31
17 | Deliverance	32
18 | Waiting Period	34
19 | To be Punctual, Committed, and Dutiful	35
20 | Intimacy with the Lord	37
21 | Rejection	38
22 | Perspective	39
23 | The Seven Spirits of God	42
24 | The Fruit of the Spirit	43
25 | Joy	44
26 | Truth	45
27 | Freedom/Liberty	46
28 | Maturity	47
29 | Who He Made You to Be	49
30 | Stability, Steadfastness, and Planted	50
About the Authors	52

1 | Salvation

Salvation is a gift. It is the display of God's compassion, sovereignty, and power through the working of His Spirit by accepting and believing His Son, Jesus Christ, is Lord of all. The sooner one comes into the knowledge of Christ and becomes a born-again believer, the sooner one will receive life and can have life more abundantly.

"The thief does not come except to steal, and to kill, and to destroy. I have come that they may have life, and that they may have *it* more abundantly." (John 10:10 NKJV)

"So they said, 'Believe on the Lord Jesus Christ, and you will be saved, you and your household.' Then they spoke the word of the Lord to him and to all who were in his house. And he took them the same hour of the night and washed *their* stripes. And immediately he and all his *family* were baptized." (Acts 16:31-33 NKJV)

"For by grace you have been saved through faith, and that not of yourselves; *it is* the gift of God, not of works, lest anyone should boast." (Ephesians 2:8-9 NKJV)

"For the wages of sin *is* death, but the gift of God *is* eternal life in Christ Jesus our Lord." (Romans 6:23 NKJV)

"that if you confess with your mouth the Lord Jesus and believe in your heart that God has raised Him from the dead, you will be saved. For with the heart one believes unto righteousness, and with the mouth, confession is made unto salvation. For the Scripture says, 'Whoever believes in Him will not be put to shame.' For there is no distinction between Jew and

Greek, for the same Lord overall is rich to all who call upon Him. For 'whoever calls on the name of the Lord shall be saved.'" (Romans 10:9-13 NKJV)

2 | Care

Take care of your spirit, soul, and body. It is the little things that go a long way. Many do not know better because they were never taught or encouraged to do so. We are spiritual beings who have a soul within a human body. We cannot just do anything with our bodies or take our bodies anywhere we want if it's not in God's will.

Our bodies do not belong to us, so we must be mindful and conscious about how we treat them. For instance, flossing and brushing your teeth every day play a role in preventing cavities.

Taking a source of vitamin D3, vitamin C, vitamin E, vitamin B12, iron, zinc, fiber, and a probiotic can assist with preventing fatigue, tiredness, bloating, inflammation, and sicknesses/diseases and improve hair, skin, and gut health. Also, doing at least 20-30 minutes of walking, stretching, eating vegetables and fruit, and drinking a lot of water is essential the older you get. But most importantly, be teachable, learn, and know what the word of God says about who you are. Any time the enemy tries to plant a seed or create a thought that tries to convince you or tell you otherwise, remember to meditate on these scriptures.

"Now may the God of peace Himself sanctify you completely; and may your whole spirit, soul, and body be preserved blameless at the coming of our Lord Jesus Christ." (1 Thessalonians 5:23 NKJV)

"Or do you not know that your body is the temple of the Holy Spirit who is in you, whom you have from God, and you are not your own? For you were bought at a

price; therefore, glorify God in your body and in your spirit, which are God's."
(1 Corinthians 6:19-20 NKJV)

"I beseech you therefore, brethren, by the mercies of God, that you present your bodies a living sacrifice, holy, acceptable to God, which is your reasonable service. And do not be conformed to this world, but be transformed by the renewing of your mind, that you may prove what is that good and acceptable and perfect will of God." (Romans 12:1-2 NKJV)

"[...]casting down arguments and every high thing that exalts itself against the knowledge of God, bringing every thought into captivity to the obedience of Christ," (2 Corinthians 10:5 NKJV)

"But I discipline my body and bring it into subjection, lest, when I have preached to others, I myself should become disqualified." (1 Corinthians 9:27 NKJV)

3 | Gifts

Gifts come without repentance. Be mindful of how you are using your gift(s). Who does it serve — the Lord, yourself, or the devil? Does it uplift, tear down, or cause separation and division in a positive way? Oftentimes, we hear people say that a person's gift *moved* them, but we should want someone's gift(s) and even our own gift(s) to *change* someone's life for the better. However, the only way a life can be changed for the better or in a more excellent way is if Christ Jesus is the focus and center.

"For the gifts and the calling of God *are* irrevocable." (Romans 11:29 NKJV)

"As each one has received a gift, minister it to one another, as good stewards of the manifold grace of God. If anyone speaks, *let him speak* as the oracles of God. If anyone ministers, *let him do it* as with the ability which God supplies, that in all things God may be glorified through Jesus Christ, to whom belong the glory and the dominion forever and ever. Amen." (1 Peter 4:10-11 NKJV)

4 | Leadership

Leadership has no age restrictions and no limitation on the appearance of an individual, and indeed these characteristics do not determine one's leadership ability. It is their heart that does. However, certain characteristics and quality traits make people great leaders. These consist of being a servant, humble, willing to continuously learn or be taught, receiving corrections/rebukes/chastisements, thinking about others (generations) and how their lives can be improved, and receiving counsel and, as a result, can give counseling to others.

"Now there was also a dispute among them, as to which of them should be considered the greatest. And He said to them, 'The kings of the Gentiles exercise lordship over them, and those who exercise authority over them are called 'benefactors.' But not so *among* you; on the contrary, he who is greatest among you, let him be as the younger, and he who governs as he who serves. For who *is* greater, he who sits at the table, or he who serves? *Is* it not he who sits at the table? Yet I am among you as the One who serves.'" (Luke 22:24-28 NKJV)

"*Let* nothing *be done* through selfish ambition or conceit, but in lowliness of mind let each esteem others better than himself." (Philippians 2:3 NKJV)

"Where *there is* no counsel, the people fall; But in the multitude of counselors *there is* safety." (Proverbs 11:14 NKJV)

"Let no one despise your youth, but be an example to the believers in word, in conduct, in love, in spirit, in faith, in purity. Till I come, give attention to reading, to

exhortation, to doctrine. Do not neglect the gift that is in you, which was given to you by prophecy with the laying on of the hands of the eldership. Meditate on these things; give yourself entirely to them, that your progress may be evident to all. Take heed to yourself and to the doctrine. Continue in them, for in doing this you will save both yourself and those who hear you." (1 Timothy 4:12-16 NKJV)

"Yes, and all who desire to live godly in Christ Jesus will suffer persecution. But evil men and impostors will grow worse and worse, deceiving and being deceived. But you must continue in the things which you have learned and been assured of, knowing from whom you have learned *them,* and that from childhood you have known the Holy Scriptures, which are able to make you wise for salvation through faith which is in Christ Jesus. All Scripture *is* given by inspiration of God, and *is* profitable for doctrine, for reproof, for correction, for instruction in righteousness, that the man of God may be complete, thoroughly equipped for every good work." (2 Timothy 3:12-17 NKJV)

"I charge *you* therefore before God and the Lord Jesus Christ, who will judge the living and the dead at His appearing and His kingdom: Preach the word! Be ready in season *and* out of season. Convince, rebuke, exhort, with all longsuffering and teaching. For the time will come when they will not endure sound doctrine, but according to their own desires, *because* they have itching ears, they will heap up for themselves teachers; and they will turn *their* ears away from the truth, and be turned aside to fables. But you be watchful in all things, endure afflictions, do the work of an evangelist, fulfill your ministry. For I am already being poured out as a drink offering, and the time of my departure is at hand. I have fought the good fight, I have finished the race, I have kept the faith. Finally, there is laid up for me the crown of righteousness, which the Lord, the righteous Judge, will give to me on that Day, and not to me only but also to all who have loved His appearing." (2 Timothy 4:1-8 NKJV)

"Remind them to be subject to rulers and authorities, to obey, to be ready for every good work, to speak evil of no one, to be peaceable, gentle, showing all humility to all men. For we ourselves were also once foolish, disobedient, deceived, serving various lusts and pleasures, living in malice and envy, hateful and hating one another. But when the kindness and the love of God our Savior toward man appeared, not by works of righteousness which we have done, but according to His mercy, He saved us, through the washing of regeneration and renewing of the Holy Spirit, whom He poured out on us abundantly through Jesus Christ our Savior, that having been justified by His grace we should become heirs according to the hope of eternal life.

This is a faithful saying, and these things I want you to affirm constantly, that those who have believed in God should be careful to maintain good works. These things are good and profitable to men." (Titus 3:1-8 NKJV)

5 | Love

Love is powerful. It doesn't fail. We can love and know love because of God. He gave us His Son, who laid down His life for our sins so we could be restored and receive eternal life.

Through Jesus' life, we see how He loved and still loves others despite their sinful actions toward Him, their unbelief in who He is, and their unwillingness to obey Him.

When we understand and know that the Lord loves us, we then learn how to love ourselves and others correctly. You can only love others to the magnitude of how you love yourself. Never put yourself down or have a self-pity spirit due to comparison or thinking you need to check off boxes to have accomplishments or goals completed by a certain age or time. Therefore, we must learn how to acknowledge and celebrate others because in order for us to be seen as righteous, we must love our neighbors as we love ourselves.

"So he answered and said, 'You shall love the Lord your God with all your heart, with all your soul, with all your strength, and with all your mind,' and 'your neighbor as yourself.'" (Luke 10:27 NKJV)

"We love Him because He first loved us." (John 4:19 NKJV)

"But above all these things put on love, which is the bond of perfection." (Colossians 3:14 NKJV)

"And now abide faith, hope, love, these three; but the greatest of these *is* love." (1 Corinthians 13:13 NKJV)

6 | Words

Words make us who and what we are. Words create and frame our life or world. You could be shaping (building, cutting, or destroying) your life or someone else's. Therefore, choose, listen, and receive words wisely.

"By faith we understand that the worlds were framed by the word of God, so that the things which are seen were not made of things which are visible." (Hebrews 11:3 NKJV)

"Indeed, we put bits in horses' mouths that they may obey us, and we turn their whole body. Look also at ships: although they are so large and are driven by fierce winds, they are turned by a very small rudder wherever the pilot desires. Even so, the tongue is a little member and boasts great things. See how great a forest a little fire kindles! And the tongue *is* a fire, a world of iniquity. The tongue is so set among our members that it defiles the whole body, and sets on fire the course of nature, and it is set on fire by hell. (James 3:3-6 NKJV)

"There is one who speaks like the piercings of a sword, But the tongue of the wise *promotes* health." (Proverbs 12:18 NKJV)

7 | Wisdom

Ask for wisdom. Age does not determine how wise you are or will become. Wisdom waits for us to accept her. There is heavenly wisdom versus demonic wisdom. God Jehovah's wisdom is heavenly, and everyone does not carry His wisdom. Heavenly wisdom is beyond the natural ability of a man to know of only things of this world according to the flesh. To have the spirit of wisdom from God is to understand and agree with heaven's plans and strategies.

Some examples of those in the Bible, but not limited to these, are as mentioned. Jesus Christ our Lord, when He was young and in the house of God, He increased in wisdom and stature, so this lets us know that wisdom can continue to grow; it never stays at just one level due to life experiences.

Joseph, one of Jacob's sons, was mature and wise at thirty years of age, and Pharoah noticed that he was. Joseph was enslaved in Egypt but was set as an overseer of Pharaoh's house due to the wisdom God had given him (*read these chapters in Genesis 39-41*). The Lord was with Joseph, and he was successful; so the wisdom of God is like one's faith; it can be seen by others and cause favor to take place in your life. Daniel and his friends also had the wisdom of God, and it was seen among men.

"Who is wise and understanding among you? Let him show by good conduct that his works are done in the meekness of wisdom. But if you have bitter envy and self-seeking in your hearts, do not boast and lie against the truth. This wisdom does not descend from above, but is earthly, sensual, demonic. For where envy and self-seeking exist, confusion and every evil thing are

there. But the wisdom that is from above is first pure, then peaceable, gentle, willing to yield, full of mercy and good fruits, without partiality and without hypocrisy. Now the fruit of righteousness is sown in peace by those who make peace." (James 3:13-18 NKJV)

"And Jesus increased in wisdom and stature, and in favor with God and men." (Luke 2:52 NKJV)

"Then Pharaoh said to Joseph, "Inasmuch as God has shown you all this, there is no one as discerning and wise as you." (Genesis 41:39 NKJV)

"As for these four young men, God gave them knowledge and skill in all literature and wisdom; and Daniel had understanding in all visions and dreams." (Daniel 1:17 NKJV)

"Be very careful, then, how you live—not as unwise but as wise, making the most of every opportunity, because the days are evil. Therefore do not be foolish, but understand what the Lord's will is. Do not get drunk on wine, which leads to debauchery. Instead, be filled with the Spirit," (Ephesians 5:15-18 NKJV)

8 | Forgiveness

A lot of God's people feel like they are stuck or are stagnant in certain areas of their life. This is often due to unforgiveness — not forgiving others or themselves.

Even when someone says they forgive someone or forgive themself, if their speech always reverts to what happened in the past and it's said with pain and hurt, or the way one acts changes when the person(s) who hurt them is mentioned, forgiveness did not fully take place.

If we don't forgive in order to be forgiven, we become an open target. Lastly, when you forgive others that does not mean you have to let them have access to you. Forgive and let go.

"And whenever you stand praying, if you have anything against anyone, forgive him, that your Father in heaven may also forgive you your trespasses. But if you do not forgive, neither will your Father in heaven forgive your trespasses." (Mark 11:25-26 NKJV)

9 | Pure in Heart

Everything flows from out of your heart. Just as our natural heart fuels our bodies with blood and oxygen, our spiritual heart conducts how we think, speak, and act. The heart is a spiritual matter, and we must keep it clean daily. Allow the word of God to cleanse your heart from the pain, anger, and frustration caused by the enemy. Jesus is the Healer! Get to know Him as such.

Always remember to repent, forgive, and release people and situations from your heart.

"Jesus said to him, 'You shall love the LORD your God with all your heart, with all your soul, and with all your mind.'" (Matthew 22:37 NKJV)

"There is one who speaks like the piercings of a sword, But the tongue of the wise *promotes* health." (Proverbs 4:23 NKJV)

"Blessed are the pure in heart, for they shall see God." (Matthew 5:8 NKJV)

"Who may ascend into the hill of the Lord? Or who may stand in His holy place? He who has clean hands and a pure heart, Who has not lifted up his soul to an idol, Nor sworn deceitfully. He shall receive blessing from the Lord, And righteousness from the God of his salvation." (Psalms 24:3-5 NKJV)

10 | Stewardship

To steward or stewardship means to be generous, wise, conduct, supervise, or manage something. It also means to be especially careful, to have responsible management of something. One can be entrusted to have stewardship over their health, property, natural resources, finances, time, or responsibilities.

For example, time and money management are vital to one's life. Neither should ever be wasted or wasteful. Due to generational blessings (wisdom) or curses, the ability to handle time and money is valuable to the kingdom of God. We must be able to effectively execute both resources in order to take care of His body (the church), which is more significant than your local church.

It is international and affects nations. To steward correctly, we must be taught and perform the principles of the kingdom of God and His ways. Always remember that it takes change (money) to make a change, so steward well over a few things, and God will cause you to increase.

"He who has a slack hand becomes poor, But the hand of the diligent makes rich." (Proverbs 10:4 NKJV)

"His Lord said to him, 'Well done, good and faithful servant; you have been faithful over a few things, I will make you ruler over many things. Enter into the joy of your Lord.'" (Matthew 25:23 NKJV)

11 | Give Thanks, Be Thankful

One of the first scriptures we ever learned was 1 Thessalonians 5:16-18. At the time, we were in high school, and a teacher of ours introduced us to it, and it has stuck with us until today. We give thanks for the little things because our situations and circumstances can always be worse than we think. We know at times, giving thanks to the Lord is difficult to do, especially when storms of life come. Everyone's storms look different, and some last longer, but when we rejoice, pray without ceasing, and give thanks, it keeps us protected and in the will of God.

"Rejoice always, pray without ceasing, in everything give thanks; for this is the will of God in Christ Jesus for you." (1 Thessalonians 5:16-18 NKJV)

"Rejoice in the Lord always. Again I will say, rejoice! Let your gentleness be known to all men. The Lord *is* at hand. Be anxious for nothing, but in everything by prayer and supplication, with thanksgiving, let your requests be made known to God; and the peace of God, which surpasses all understanding, will guard your hearts and minds through Christ Jesus." (Philippians 4:4-7 NKJV)

12 | Covetousness, Envy, and Jealousy

Comparison kills, even when done a little bit. It often kills our dreams before they even get started. The spirit of covetousness causes one to have an excessive desire and lust for wealth or possessions and can sometimes mean to desire for another person's possessions. The spirit of envy causes one to feel discontent and a desire to have an attribute or achievement that belongs to someone else because they lack it. The spirit of jealousy causes one to be angry because they do not have what someone else has spiritually, naturally, or financially.

To make it plain, all three spirits have a common theme: the desire to have something that someone else has. If you have any of these spirits, get delivered. The Lord allows you to identify these spirits so you won't become an adulterer, fornicator, murderer, or thief spiritually, naturally, and or financially. But if someone attacks you who has these spirits, be assured that it is God's will for them to push you into what He has for you.

"For from within, out of the heart of men, proceed evil thoughts, adulteries, fornications, murders, thefts, covetousness, wickedness, deceit, lewdness, an evil eye, blasphemy, pride, foolishness." (Mark 7:21-22 NKJV)

"Therefore put to death your members which are on the earth: fornication, uncleanness, passion, evil desire, and covetousness, which is idolatry." (Colossians 3:5 NKJV)

"A sound heart *is* life to the body, But envy *is* rottenness to the bones." (Proverbs 14:30 NKJV)

"[…]Jealousy *as* cruel as the grave; Its flames *are* flames of fire, A most vehement flame." (Song of Solomon 8:6 NKJV)

13 | Our Circle

Who we associate and surround ourselves with influences and defines us. Even though there were many people around Jesus, they did not know the moves He would make or the Father's perfect will for His life unless He chose to disclose the information. Jesus also had twelve disciples, but His inner circle consisted of three, Peter, James, and John, so He could pour into them what they would need to stand firm. Be wise when choosing your inner circle; it determines your personal and financial growth.

"Blessed *is* the man Who walks not in the counsel of the ungodly, Nor stands in the path of sinners, Nor sits in the seat of the scornful[...]" (Psalms 1:1 NKJV)

"Can two walk together, unless they are agreed?" (Amos 3:3 NKJV)

"Again I say to you that if two of you agree on earth concerning anything that they ask, it will be done for them by My Father in heaven. For where two or three are gathered together in My name, I am there in the midst of them." (Matthew 18:19-20 NKJV)

14 | Healing

Healing is to make one healthy, whole, or sound; restore to health; free from illness, disease, torment, or bondage.

Jesus heals. He is the Lord God, our healer (*Jehovah Rapha*). Healing makes us complete, well, and whole. We all need healing in certain areas of our lives, whether we admit it or not. Jesus can heal every area in our lives; healing can take place spiritually, naturally, or financially.

Sicknesses, diseases, poverty, and lack occur in our lives due to a lack of knowledge, disobedience, or because of a generational curse. As witnesses to many miraculous healings and recipients of God's healing power, never be ashamed or have unbelief of this grace He freely gives to us. God shows no partiality or favoritism. He heals those whom He chooses, and it is all done for His glory.

"And Jesus went about all Galilee, teaching in their synagogues, preaching the gospel of the kingdom, and healing all kinds of sickness and all kinds of disease among the people." (Matthew 4:23 NKJV)

"But when the multitudes knew *it*, they followed Him; and He received them and spoke to them about the kingdom of God, and healed those who had need of healing." (Luke 9:11 NKJV)

"For the man was over forty years old on whom this miracle of healing had been performed." (Acts 4:22 NKJV)

"[...]how God anointed Jesus of Nazareth with the Holy Spirit and with power, who went about doing good and

healing all who were oppressed by the devil, for God was with Him." (Acts 10:38 NKJV)

15 | Tithes and Offering

Tithing was before the law. Abraham, the father of faith, gave tithes to king Melchizedek to bless God. Out of our naivety, the two of us did not know the true meaning of what tithes and offering entailed. We were cursed unknowingly, walking around with money but could never keep or grow it to store it up and limited with our blessings. Take heed to this instructional warning, and do not rob God because there are consequences that you bring on to yourself. Bring all the tithes to the storehouse, which is the Church. Many are living under a closed heaven–unaware that they are being oppressed by the spirit of lack, need, or want. It is a poverty mindset and a lie to think that giving to the Lord will cause you to lack.

We can never outgive God by what He does for us; even if we try, He will outgive us every time with anything He chooses to give us. Giving is warfare in the kingdom of God, and Satan does not want us to know how to defeat him (the devourer, cankerworm, or locust). Tithing is only 10% of our gross income or any monetary gain (gift, etc.), and we give for our own benefit and protection from the evil one.

Now your offering is free will. It blesses us. A closed hand will never receive, but one that is open cannot contain such blessings. The Lord does not give a command for how much to give as an offering in the house of God, but our giving is a sign of reverence and worship and spiritually shows our trust/faith in Jesus Christ as our Lord and Savior.

"Will a man rob God? Yet you have robbed Me! But you say, 'In what way have we robbed You?' In tithes and offerings. You are cursed with a curse, for you have

robbed Me, even this whole nation. Bring all the tithes into the storehouse, that there may be food in My house, and try Me now in this, says the Lord of hosts, 'If I will not open for you the windows of heaven and pour out for you such blessing that there will not be room enough to receive it. And I will rebuke the devourer for your sakes, so that he will not destroy the fruit of your ground, nor shall the vine fail to bear fruit for you in the field,' says the Lord of hosts." (Malachi 3:8-11 NKJV)

"Then Jesus said to His disciples, 'Assuredly, I say to you that it is hard for a rich man to enter the kingdom of heaven.'" (Matthew 19:23 NKJV)

16 | Sowing (Giving)

The Lord loves a cheerful giver. Sowing a seed financially, your time, gifts, counsel, joy, love, peace, etc., are all a form of giving. It is always better to give than it is to receive. We think that it blesses the recipient because they are in need, but in actuality, it is for the giver who is in need of something. The Lord blesses the giver whose heart is clean and gives out of a righteous motive. The recipient is only blessed with what has been given unto them. Be a sower and watch how Jesus Christ will do supernatural miracles and manifestations in your life because you have the heart to give.

"But this *I say:* He who sows sparingly will also reap sparingly, and he who sows bountifully will also reap bountifully. *So let* each one *give* as he purposes in his heart, not grudgingly or of necessity; for God loves a cheerful giver. And God *is* able to make all grace abound toward you, that you, always having all sufficiency in all *things,* may have an abundance for every good work. As it is written: 'He has dispersed abroad, He has given to the poor; His righteousness endures forever.' Now may He who supplies seed to the sower, and bread for food, supply and multiply the seed you have *sown* and increase the fruits of your righteousness," (2 Corinthians 9:6-10 NKJV)

"Give, and it will be given to you: good measure, pressed down, shaken together, and running over will be put into your bosom. For with the same measure that you use, it will be measured back to you." (Luke 6:38 NKJV)

17 | Deliverance

Depart from a life of sin, unholiness, and darkness. We have learned throughout our time as born-again believers in Jesus Christ that many people simply just do not want the word of God. They seek after energy, vibes, vibrations, magic, sage, chakras, crystals, Greek gods/goddesses, astrology, horoscopes, angel numbers, witchcraft, psychics, palm readings, tarot card readings, fortune telling, ancestral worship, root working, new age movement, religion, secret societies, cults, or man-made doctrine, fornication, lust, drugs, alcohol, adultery, etc., to try to fill the void of the Holy Trinity's rightful place. These things are demonic ideologies and practices from Satan, causing many to be in bondage while they continually search for, but never find, peace, love, or deliverance from what is holding them back from prospering in life.

These things are not equal or even a substitute for knowing God the Father. The only way to God is through His Son — Jesus Christ, the true and living God. We pray and intercede for our generation and generations to come that they will come to know the knowledge of Christ and discern what they give themselves access to. We also intercede for deliverance and the denouncing/renouncing of such covenants or soul ties to darkness to take place all over the earth.

"Now then, we are ambassadors for Christ, as though God were pleading through us: we implore you on Christ's behalf, be reconciled to God." (2 Corinthians 5:20 NKJV)

"Then, when desire has conceived, it gives birth to sin; and sin, when it is full-grown, brings forth death." (James 1:15 NKJV)

"Jesus said to him, 'I am the way, the truth, and the life. No one comes to the Father except through Me.'" (John 14:6 NKJV)

"When you come into the land which the Lord your God is giving you, you shall not learn to follow the abominations of those nations. There shall not be found among you anyone who makes his son or his daughter pass through the fire, or one who practices witchcraft, or a soothsayer, or one who interprets omens, or a sorcerer, or one who conjures spells, or a medium, or a spiritist, or one who calls up the dead. For all who do these things are an abomination to the Lord, and because of these abominations the Lord your God drives them out from before you. You shall be blameless before the Lord your God. For these nations which you will dispossess listened to soothsayers and diviners; but as for you, the Lord your God has not appointed such for you." (Deuteronomy 18:9-14 NKJV)

18 | Waiting Period

Don't awaken love until its appointed time. This applies to both women and men. Many awaken what they think is love before its time. This leads to open doors spiritually to lusting, rejection, hurt, controlling, manipulation, and sorrow, just to name a few.

Waiting on the Lord to perform His plan is key to our destiny in life. When we try to take matters into our own hands, destruction can take place, but our loving God provides His grace and mercy upon us. We want to introduce the waiting period as a precious time to draw close to the Holy Spirit and to learn who you are before trying to learn who your husband or wife may be. God already knows who He desires us to marry, and He knows what the marriage shall build as it brings glory to His kingdom.

"I charge you, O daughters of Jerusalem, do not stir up nor awaken love until it pleases." (Song of Solomon 8:4 NKJV)

"He who finds a wife finds a good thing, And obtains favor from the Lord." (Proverbs 18:22 NKJV)

"Therefore what God has joined together, let not man separate." (Mark 10:9 NKJV)

"For I know the thoughts that I think toward you, says the Lord, thoughts of peace and not of evil, to give you a future and a hope." (Jeremiah 29:11 NKJV)

19 | To be Punctual, Committed, and Dutiful

Remember, in all that you do, that literally means everything you do, do it as if you are doing it unto the Lord. We used to think we could halfway do things or do them nonchalantly if we did not enjoy them. But to be a Christian means, you lead by example in all aspects of your life. Not just some parts of your life or the parts that you think or even man thinks is cool.

We are telling you from experience. Don't make the process harder and longer due to being prideful, stubborn, or disobedient. Every day you get up, give God glory and praise; you could have been somewhere else that is far worse.

Ask the Lord for wisdom and for Him to open up your understanding in regard to why you are where you are and what it is that you need to get while you are there so you can grow into the man or woman He has called you to be.

When we are out of place, not working where and how the Lord desires us to, and not in God's timing, we risk causing someone else to miss what the Lord has for them.

Punctual - means being on time—strict observance in keeping engagements: prompt

Committed - means having promised to be involved with a plan, loyal and willing to give your time to something you confessed you would

Dutiful - means motivated by duty rather than desire or enthusiasm, obediently fulfilling one's duty

"Let all things be done decently and in order." (1 Corinthians 14:40 NKJV)

"The lazy *man* will not plow because of winter; He will beg during harvest and *have* nothing." (Proverbs 20:4 NKJV)

"The soul of a lazy *man* desires, and *has* nothing; But the soul of the diligent shall be made rich." (Proverbs 13:4 NKJV)

"And whatever you do, do it heartily, as to the Lord and not to men, knowing that from the Lord you will receive the reward of the inheritance; for you serve the Lord Christ." (Colossians 3:23-24 NKJV)

20 | Intimacy with the Lord

Intimacy means a close, familiar, and usually affectionate or loving personal relationship with another person or group. It also means to have a close association with or detailed knowledge or deep understanding of a place, subject, period of history, etc.

Our relationship development with the Lord starts in our bedrooms or favorite dwelling places. To be intimate with the Lord requires us to pray, fast, read God's word, and spend time learning how to be led by the Holy Spirit. The Holy Spirit teaches us about Christ and His character and reveals to us what we must change or correct so we can be like Him to enter into God's presence.

Intimacy with the Lord also requires separation. A time of separation allows us to know and learn how the Lord communicates with us.

"He who has My commandments and keeps them, it is he who loves Me. And he who loves Me will be loved by My Father, and I will love him and manifest Myself to him." (John 14:21 NKJV)

"Abide in Me, and I in you. As the branch cannot bear fruit of itself, unless it abides in the vine, neither can you, unless you abide in Me." (John 15:4 NKJV)

21 | Rejection

The spirit of rejection occurs when a person or group excludes an individual and refuses to acknowledge or accept them, refusing to believe someone or something.

Rejection is inevitable. Rejection happens to everyone and can come from anyone or anywhere. You can be rejected by a sports team, scholarship committee, college program, schools, internships, career/job opportunities, parents, grandparents, aunts, uncles, cousins, so-called friends, or even someone who does not even know you. Jesus Christ was rejected, so who are we to think that we are exempt?

It is all a part of the believer's life. It doesn't feel good, but it's absolutely necessary.

"You are coming to Christ, who is the living cornerstone of God's temple. He was rejected by people, but he was chosen by God for great honor." (1 Peter 2:4 NLT)

"But Jesus said to them, 'A prophet is not without honor except in his own country, among his own relatives, and in his own house.'" (Mark 6:4 NKJV)

22 | Perspective

How we see ourselves matters. We are seated in heavenly places. Meaning we are placed up high, so the things we see do not appear as they are (big, scary, dreadful, etc.). Sometimes age plays a huge factor, and it prevents us from seeing correctly because of past failures and fear. However, we must learn to see out of the eyes of Christ and ask the Holy Spirit if we are in the right position because He will lead us to it if we are not. Lastly, how we see ourselves impacts not only ourselves but generations. For instance, Joshua and Caleb did not see themselves as grasshoppers and believed that the Lord would do what He said because of their belief and obedience.

"Then Caleb quieted the people before Moses, and said, 'Let us go up at once and take possession, for we are well able to overcome it.' But the men who had gone up with him said, 'We are not able to go up against the people, for they *are* stronger than we.' And they gave the children of Israel a bad report of the land which they had spied out, saying, 'The land through which we have gone as spies *is* a land that devours its inhabitants, and all the people whom we saw in it *are* men of *great* stature. There we saw the giants (the descendants of Anak came from the giants); and we were like grasshoppers in our own sight, and so we were in their sight.'" (Numbers 13:30-33 NKJV)

"So all the congregation lifted up their voices and cried, and the people wept that night. And all the children of Israel complained against Moses and Aaron, and the whole congregation said to them, 'If only we had died in the land of Egypt! Or if only we had died in this wilderness! Why has the Lord brought us to this land to fall by the sword, that our wives and children should

become victims? Would it not be better for us to return to Egypt?' So they said to one another, 'Let us select a leader and return to Egypt.' Then Moses and Aaron fell on their faces before all the assembly of the congregation of the children of Israel. But Joshua the son of Nun and Caleb the son of Jephunneh, *who were* among those who had spied out the land, tore their clothes; and they spoke to all the congregation of the children of Israel, saying: 'The land we passed through to spy out *is* an exceedingly good land. If the Lord delights in us, then He will bring us into this land and give it to us, a land which flows with milk and honey. Only do not rebel against the Lord, nor fear the people of the land, for they *are* our bread; their protection has departed from them, and the Lord *is* with us. Do not fear them.' And all the congregation said to stone them with stones. Now the glory of the Lord appeared in the tabernacle of meeting before all the children of Israel.

And the Lord spoke to Moses and Aaron, saying, 'How long *shall I bear with* this evil congregation who complain against Me? I have heard the complaints which the children of Israel make against Me. Say to them, as I live,' says the Lord, 'Just as you have spoken in My hearing, so I will do to you: The carcasses of you who have complained against Me shall fall in this wilderness, all of you who were numbered, according to your entire number, from twenty years old and above. Except for Caleb the son of Jephunneh and Joshua the son of Nun, you shall by no means enter the land which I swore I would make you dwell in. But your little ones, whom you said would be victims, I will bring in, and they shall know the land which you have despised. But *as for* you, your carcasses shall fall in this wilderness.'

Now the men whom Moses sent to spy out the land, who returned and made all the congregation complain against him by bringing a bad report of the land, those very men who brought the evil report about the land, died by the plague before the Lord. But Joshua the son of Nun and Caleb the son of Jephunneh remained alive, of the men who went to spy out the land." (Numbers 14:1-10, 26-32, 36-38 NKJV)

23 | The Seven Spirits of God

The seven Spirits of God are vital to have as a born-again believer. At first, we may not possess all seven, but we can ask the Lord for them and grow from level to level in them. The seven Spirits of God help us in our everyday lives. They assist us when making decisions, when needing to create something, and how we must conduct ourselves in our speech and behavior, especially when dealing with people.

"There shall come forth a Rod from the stem of Jesse, And a Branch shall grow out of his roots. The Spirit of the Lord shall rest upon Him, The Spirit of wisdom and understanding, The Spirit of counsel and might, The Spirit of knowledge and of the fear of the Lord." (Isaiah 11:1-2 NKJV)

24 | The Fruit of the Spirit

The fruit of the Spirit is like an orange. We must have all nine slices to possess the fruit of the Spirit fully. The fruit of the Spirit can be seen in a believer's life if they bear it, and it is vital in terms of keeping believers in the perfect will of God spiritually, naturally, and financially. Check off the ones you do have, then pray and ask the Lord to give you the ones you do not possess so you may grow in them all to contain the whole fruit of the Spirit.

"But the fruit of the Spirit is love, joy, peace, longsuffering, kindness, goodness, faithfulness, gentleness, self-control. Against such there is no law. And those who are Christ's have crucified the flesh with its passions and desires. If we live in the Spirit, let us also walk in the Spirit. Let us not become conceited, provoking one another, envying one another." (Galatians 5:22-26 NKJV)

25 | Joy

The Bible tells us numerous times that God gives us joy and peace. It tells us that real joy comes from God and is ours forever. Fun is not equivalent to the joy of the Lord. Fun is the world's counterfeit to Godly joy. Satan does not create anything, so to deceive the Lord's people, Satan, the adversary, will cause many who are not saved to think a night out committing sin is considered joyous. The joy of the Lord is experienced at all times, even in the midst of tests and trials; it can never be taken away unless we allow the enemy to take it from us. Joy is a weapon in our supernatural arsenal, and we pray that just like we have received the joy of the Lord, you too will receive it as a gift from God and never let it go.

"The joy of the Lord is your strength." (Nehemiah 8:10 NKJV)

"These things I have spoken to you, that My joy may remain in you, and *that* your joy may be full." (John 15:11 NKJV)

"To console those who mourn in Zion, to give them beauty for ashes, the oil of joy for mourning, the garment of praise for the spirit of heaviness[...]" (Isaiah 61:3 NKJV)

"[…]for the kingdom of God is not eating and drinking, but righteousness and peace and joy in the Holy Spirit." (Romans 14:17 NKJV)

26 | Truth

Speak, teach, tell, and walk in the truth. The truth is the gospel of Jesus Christ. Our decision to do so is the only way people can be made free. The truth hurts to hear and read sometimes, but it causes one to grow or to move past a situation or circumstance. The Lord came to tell us who we are and redeemed us back to the Father through the remission of our sins. Those who receive this are made free spiritually, naturally, and financially.

"Then Jesus said to those Jews who believed Him, 'If you abide in My word, you are My disciples indeed. And you shall know the truth, and the truth shall make you free.' They answered Him, 'We are Abraham's descendants, and have never been in bondage to anyone. How *can* You say, 'You will be made free?' Jesus answered them, 'Most assuredly, I say to you, whoever commits sin is a slave of sin. And a slave does not abide in the house forever, *but* a son abides forever. Therefore if the Son makes you free, you shall be free indeed.'" (John 8:31-36 NKJV)

"Jesus said to him, 'I am the way, the truth, and the life. No one comes to the Father except through Me.'" (John 14:6 NKJV)

27 | Freedom/Liberty

We can be made free in Christ Jesus. His word alone, if we receive it, makes us free in our souls and our minds. Freedom in Christ does not mean you are able to do anything you want however you want. Freedom in Christ means you are no longer bound by pain, hurt, and suffering. You no longer willingly commit sin (think in error --- fearfully/doubt, drink, smoke, lay and or play, etc.) to "escape" your reality or present situations and circumstances. To be free in Christ means we can see ourselves and other people just like Christ does, and we can genuinely love no matter how we have been treated or mishandled.

"For you, brethren, have been called to liberty; only do not *use* liberty as an opportunity for the flesh, but through love serve one another." (Galatians 5:13 NKJV)

"Now the Lord is the Spirit; and where the Spirit of the Lord *is*, there is liberty." (2 Corinthians 3:17 NKJV)

"[...]as free, yet not using liberty as a cloak for vice, but as bondservants of God. Honor all *people.* Love the brotherhood. Fear God. Honor the king." (1 Peter 2:16-17 NKJV)

"The Spirit of the Lord God is upon me, because the Lord has anointed me to preach good tidings to the poor; He has sent me to heal the brokenhearted, to proclaim liberty to the captives, and the opening of the prison to those who are bound." (Isaiah 61:1 NKJV)

28 | Maturity

Knowing the difference between good and evil and choosing to do what is good (or right) at all times is maturity. Maturity is also being able to listen, knowing when to speak, and how to speak. We all must give an account for what we have done and will do in this life while on the earth. Nothing we do is hidden from the Lord. He knows all and sees all – He is omnipresent.

Living a life that does not line up with the word of God is exposed and seen by the Lord. Even the hidden sins, (iniquity and transgressions) are all seen and known by God. Our inner thoughts and desires — for all of these we must give an account. But by the grace and goodness of our mighty deliverer, Jesus Christ, we can learn to live a life of holiness and righteousness. This comes through salvation and a life fully submitted unto Jesus and His word.

"For the word of God is alive and powerful. It is sharper than the sharpest two-edged sword, cutting between soul and spirit, between joint and marrow. It exposes our innermost thoughts and desires. Nothing in all creation is hidden from God. Everything is naked and exposed before his eyes, and he is the one to whom we are accountable." (Peter 4:12-13 NLT)

"Therefore, laying aside all malice, all deceit, hypocrisy, envy, and all evil speaking, as newborn babes, desire the pure milk of the word, that you may grow thereby, if indeed you have tasted that the Lord is gracious." (1 Peter 2:1-2 NKJV)

"Who is the man who desires life, And loves many days, that he may see good? Keep your tongue from evil, And

your lips from speaking deceit. Depart from evil and do good; Seek peace and pursue it. The eyes of the Lord are on the righteous, And His ears are open to their cry. The face of the Lord is against those who do evil, To cut off the remembrance of them from the earth." (Psalms 34:12-16 NKJV)

"But solid food is for the mature, who by constant use have trained themselves to distinguish good from evil." (Hebrews 5:14 NIV)

29 | Who He Made You to Be

Beloved, you are fearfully and wonderfully made. Sometimes the Lord reveals to us, our leaders, or even to our family members who we are and what our calling is. This is done however He wills and pleases to do so. The way we look physically, the activities we participated in as children, and even our experiences are for a time and purpose. He knows every intricate detail and component about us: our stature, voice, appearance (hair, eyes, skin, etc.), anointing, gifts, and more because He knew beforehand who we are called to be.

All of us are not meant to look the same or act the same, which to us is amazing because God literally took His time to create everyone, just like an artist does when creating a masterpiece. With that being said, we are designed exactly how our Master, Jesus Christ, created us to be from our mother's wombs. Through this life, we change or adapt over the years. His goodness and deepest love for us is what causes us to understand that He knows us closely, deep down to our own personality traits and callings. Be at peace with how you were made to be and delight in the grace He has given you to share His goodness and glory.

"I will praise You, for I am fearfully and wonderfully made; marvelous are Your works, and that my soul knows very well." (Psalms 139:14 NKJV)

"Everyone who is called by My name, Whom I have created for My glory; I have formed him, yes, I have made him." (Isaiah 43:7 NKJV)

30 | Stability, Steadfastness, and Planted

Stability, steadfastness, and being planted can be defined as the quality of being unchanging, and constancy of character or purpose. Therefore, stay in God's perfect will once you are in it. Even though there are times when we may feel that we may not have obtained certain things by a specific age, stay the course. Stability is being faithful to God and not to man.

Steadfastness in life also means you are planted or rooted in a place, and in that place is where you can grow and be watered. In this generation, many are so quick to uproot themselves and go with their feelings and desires, or to allow a job to take them without consulting the Lord about His will. When we do this, it causes us to be unstable. Instability means uncertainty and the liability to give way or to fail in character or purpose. Instability causes us to be in a place of no protection or covering from situations and storms that we do not know are plotted by the enemy.

We fight against instability by desiring and asking the Lord for His wisdom and knowledge. We also fight against instability by sticking to God's plan, holding on to what we have been taught, and doing what we have read and seen, which is truth (the gospel of Jesus Christ).

"He shall be like a tree planted by the rivers of water, that brings forth its fruit in its season, whose leaf also shall not wither; and whatever he does shall prosper." (Psalms 1:3 NKJV)

"Those who are planted in the house of the Lord Shall flourish in the courts of our God." (Psalms 92:13 NKJV)

"Therefore, beloved, looking forward to these things, be diligent to be found by Him in peace, without spot and blameless; and consider *that* the longsuffering of our Lord *is* salvation—as also our beloved brother Paul, according to the wisdom given to him, has written to you, as also in all his epistles, speaking in them of these things, in which are some things hard to understand, which untaught and unstable *people* twist to their own destruction, as *they do* also the rest of the Scriptures. You therefore, beloved, since you know *this* beforehand, beware lest you also fall from your own steadfastness, being led away with the error of the wicked; but grow in the grace and knowledge of our Lord and Savior Jesus Christ. To Him *be* the glory both now and forever. Amen."(2 Peter 3:14-18 NKJV)

"Wisdom and knowledge will be the stability of your times, *And* the strength of salvation; The fear of the Lord *is* His treasure." (Isaiah 33:6 NKJV)

"[…]that they may be called trees of righteousness, the planting of the Lord, that He may be glorified." (Isaiah 61:3 NKJV)

About the Authors

Dr. Amber Goodman and Dr. Ashley Goodman are known for their unique and tailored writing styles of concise yet impactful, easily digestible, and detailed content for their target audiences. They are now the authors of four books: *A Double Portion to Know Him, The Outcast Pharmacist, Abba Father & Me: A Daily Devotional, and 30 Things: Twin Tells.* Drs. Amber and Ashley are a dynamic duo of emerging young leaders, prophetesses, and college professors. Their church home for spiritual training and equipping is Heaven to Earth Worship Center in Tampa, FL.

As a result of their upbringing, academics and athletics have molded these two into the leaders they are today. Both received full scholarships to play basketball in addition to receiving academic scholarships. After basketball concluded, their vision was set to become doctors of pharmacy. Their faith in Jesus Christ, along with a love for the apostolic and prophetic, has led them to accept the call as five-fold ministers and to further their education within the fields of public health and business administration.

As growing figureheads in healthcare with a passion for full-time ministry, they are determined to influence the quality of healthcare delivery and systems for generations to come. With this spiritual mandate, both aspire to bring light to those who are in darkness, helping others discover salvation and their place in God's perfect will. Drs. Ashley and Amber plan to continue imparting revelations of the Lord through the spirits of knowledge, wisdom, and counsel.

To learn more about them or to connect with them, please visit www.goodmantwins.com.

www.ingramcontent.com/pod-product-compliance
Lightning Source LLC
Chambersburg PA
CBHW070210100426
42743CB00013B/3121